THIS
Book
BELONGS TO

_____

For my husband and children,
thank you for your love and support!

First Edition: May 2021
Second Edition: March 2022

Written by L.R. Hanson
Self-Published

ISBN: 9798500675583

Winter Survival

animal hibernation, migration, and adaptation

SECOND EDITION

by L.R. HANSON

In December, the winter air feels cold.

Dried fallen leaves on the ground start to mold.

Animals start to prepare for winter in different ways.

Beavers can adapt to winter because they have a thick and waterproof coat to keep them warm and dry. They live in strong lodges built with sticks, dry grass, and mud. The entrance is under the water, away from predators. They eat barks from trees that they have stored away during the warmer months. Beavers have a tail that store fat and help them regulate their body temperature.

Some animals will leave their habitat, while some will stay.

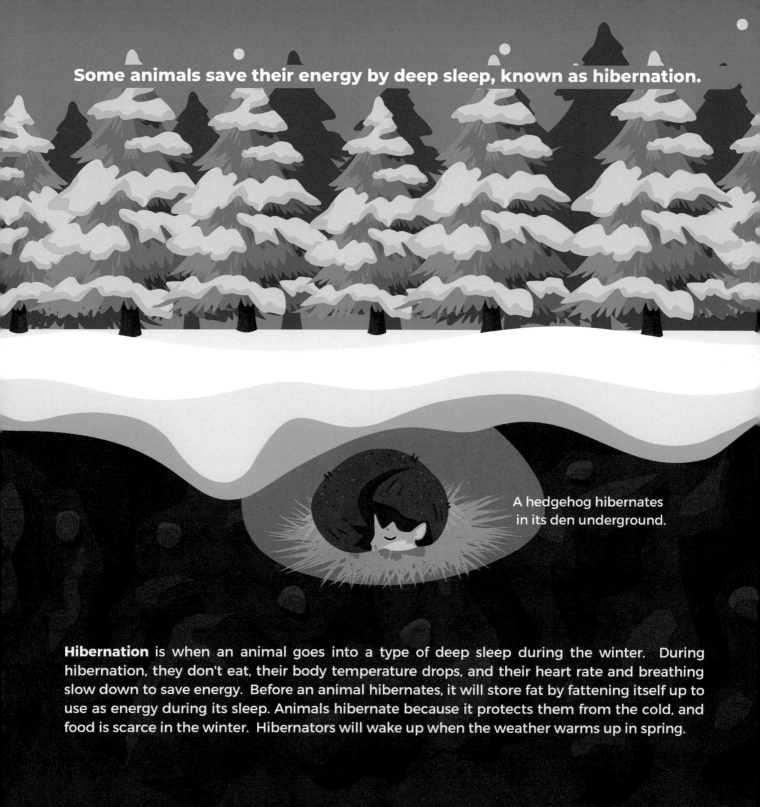

Some animals save their energy by deep sleep, known as hibernation.

A hedgehog hibernates in its den underground.

Hibernation is when an animal goes into a type of deep sleep during the winter. During hibernation, they don't eat, their body temperature drops, and their heart rate and breathing slow down to save energy. Before an animal hibernates, it will store fat by fattening itself up to use as energy during its sleep. Animals hibernate because it protects them from the cold, and food is scarce in the winter. Hibernators will wake up when the weather warms up in spring.

Some animals travel south to avoid the cold, known as migration.

Caribous migrate south for winter in large herds.

Migration is when animals travel from one habitat to another in search of food, a warmer climate, or to breed. Animals migrate at certain times of the year and they usually travel long distances to reach their destination. Many animals that migrate during the winter include caribous, birds, whales, and insects.

Animals that change their bodies and behaviors are known as adaptation.

Adaptation is any behavioral or physical changes in animals that have evolved over generations to help them survive in their habitat. Polar bears have developed two layers of fur and a thick layer of fat as insulation to keep them warm in the cold arctic climate. Their fur is white to camouflage themselves from their prey on the snow and ice.

Snakes coil tightly together to stay warm and go into deep brumation.

Brumation is like hibernation, but for cold-blooded animals, like reptiles and amphibians. During brumation, their activity, heart rate, temperature, and respiratory rate drop. They are in deep sleep but will move around on warmer winter days. Snakes will hide under rocks or in burrows to stay warm and safe.

Squirrels are busy gathering nuts by stuffing their cheeks.

Tree squirrels are adaptive to winter and do not hibernate. In the fall, they will gather food and store it away. They will fatten themselves up to build up fat reserves. The reserves will be used as energy throughout the winter, and the extra layer of fat helps keep them warm. They are active throughout the winter, running around fetching the food they have hidden away.

Frogs and turtles hide under rocks or logs along the creeks.

Frogs and turtles brumate in the winter. Frogs hide around ponds, under rocks, or deep in the mud to avoid freezing. Some frog species can be partially frozen and will still survive. They produce a high level of glucose, a type of sugar, in their bodies that acts like antifreeze, preventing their organs from freezing over. They may appear frozen and dead, but they will thaw themselves out when the temperature rises. Turtles usually brumate at the bottom of ponds, lakes, or deep under the mud. Their body temperature and heart rate drop, they don't eat, and they need less oxygen to survive. They have a special ability to get oxygen from the water and do not need to come up for air.

Geese fly south in groups, making a V-shaped line in a single file.

Canada geese migrate to the south during the winter. They fly in a V-shaped formation, with one leader in the front and the rest of the flock following behind. The "V" formation helps lift and reduces drag, so the geese can save energy, fly longer, and fly with better coordination.

Whales search for warmer waters by swimming for many miles.

Humpback whales migrate to the south in the winter to more tropical waters near the equator to give birth and nurse their calves. They do not feed during winter migration. They will eat again when they journey back to the nutrient-rich waters in the north.

Mice collect and save food during the fall to eat it later.

Mice remain active during the winter and do not hibernate. In the fall, they gather food and stash it away to eat it later. They will search for food during winter, but will stay inside on very cold days. They burrow deep below the ground or might even take shelter in houses behind drywall, in attics, or anywhere safe, warm, and dry.

Rabbits grow thick white fur, blending into their surrounding nature.

Rabbits are adaptive and do not hibernate in the winter. They are active all year-round, searching for bark, bush buds, and twigs to eat. They stay warm by growing a thicker coat of fur in the fall. Their fur coats will also change to a lighter shade to protect them from predators. Some rabbit's fur can turn completely white, camouflaging them in the snow and ice.

Monarch butterflies fly down south for a warmer climate.

Every year, the monarch butterfly makes the long journey from Canada and the US to the forest in central Mexico to hibernate. During hibernation, they are fairly inactive to save energy. They hibernate in large clusters in oyamel fir trees to keep warm. In March, they will return to the north to lay their eggs on milkweed flowers.

Bear sleeps while the outside temperature is in the minus.

Bears hibernate in the winter. During hibernation, their body temperature lowers, their heart rate and breathing decreases, and they do not eat, drink, or pass waste. To prepare for hibernation, they eat many pounds of food to bulk up. They make their dens in hollow trees, rock crevices, or caves. Bears don't always sleep throughout their hibernation. Pregnant bears will wake up to give birth before going back to sleep until spring.

Winter days are short, while nights are long with snowy storms.

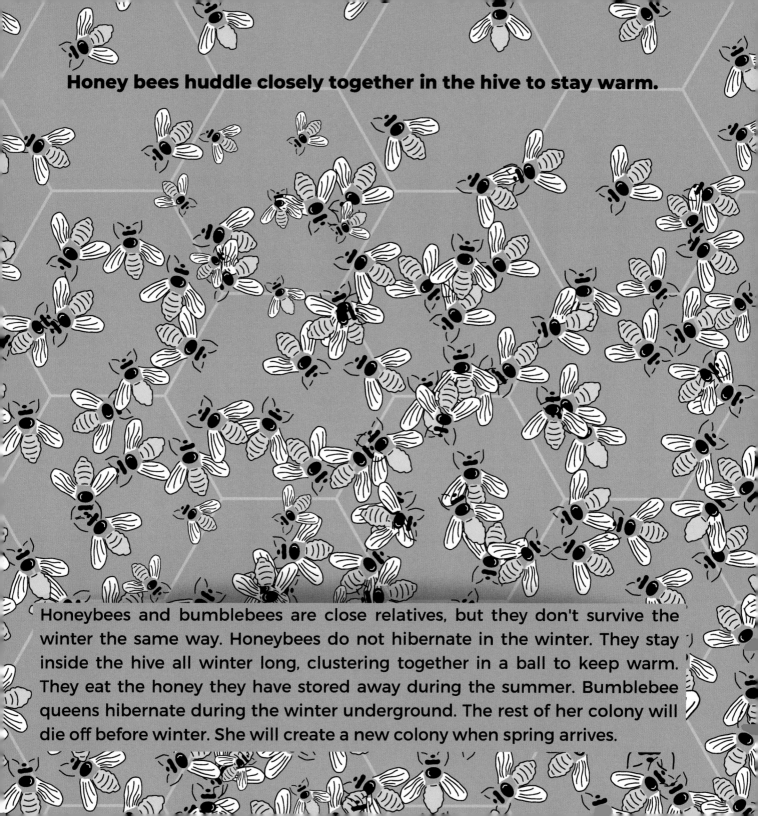

Honey bees huddle closely together in the hive to stay warm.

Honeybees and bumblebees are close relatives, but they don't survive the winter the same way. Honeybees do not hibernate in the winter. They stay inside the hive all winter long, clustering together in a ball to keep warm. They eat the honey they have stored away during the summer. Bumblebee queens hibernate during the winter underground. The rest of her colony will die off before winter. She will create a new colony when spring arrives.

Bats live off stored fat and slow down their heartbeat.
Their body temperature drops, and they will not eat.

Some bat species hibernate, some migrate, and some do both. During hibernation, bats can survive without food for a long time by reducing their heart rate, body temperature, and breathing. They live off the stored fat in their bodies. Bats stay warm in places like dark caves, rock crevices, mines, and other ideal structures. Some bat species migrate in the winter because food supply becomes scarce or they want to find ideal habitats for hibernating.

Fox leaps and dives headfirst into the snow to catch mice.

Foxes do not hibernate in the winter because they are adaptive to the cold with their thick fur coats. Hunting for food in the winter becomes difficult, so they need to be clever when hunting. Foxes have excellent hearing and can detect their prey scurrying underneath the snow-covered ground. They will track and pounce, diving headfirst into the snow to catch their meal.

Fishes stay warm on the bottom under the lake ice.

Freshwater fishes don't hibernate in the winter, but they slow down their activity. They often gather in groups near the bottom of lakes where the water temperature is warmer to take a rest. Their heart rate slows down, they don't move or eat much, and their need for oxygen decreases.

Earthworms stay cozy and are inactive below the ground.

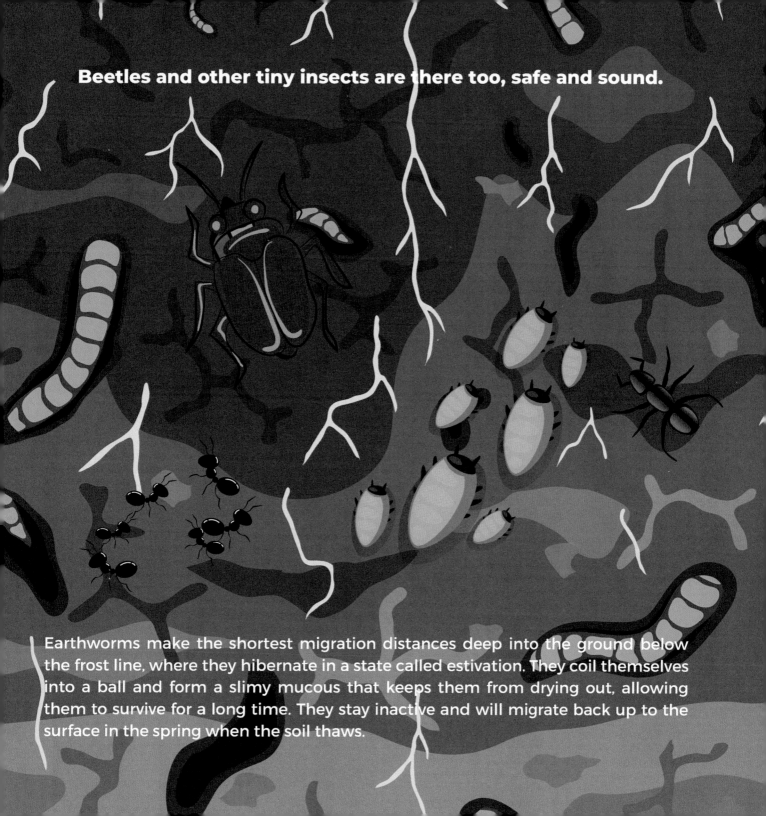

Beetles and other tiny insects are there too, safe and sound.

Earthworms make the shortest migration distances deep into the ground below the frost line, where they hibernate in a state called estivation. They coil themselves into a ball and form a slimy mucous that keeps them from drying out, allowing them to survive for a long time. They stay inactive and will migrate back up to the surface in the spring when the soil thaws.

Deer spends winter looking for mosses, twigs, barks, and leaves to eat.

Whitetail deers do not hibernate in the winter, but they will slow down their activity. Deers will forage for food in the snow for twigs, berries, bark, mosses, and other food. On very cold days, they will conserve energy by keeping still in shelters beneath pine trees. Pine trees have low branches with needles that protect them from the snow, rain, and wind. They will also grow a thick fur coat in the fall to keep them warm throughout the winter.

Wolf's tail covers its nose and with his breath, warms his feet by creating heat.

Wolves are active in the winter and do not hibernate. Wolves are adaptive to cold temperatures, thanks to their thick fur coat. Their fur coat consists of two layers, guard hairs for the outer layer and an undercoat layer underneath. The guard hairs are long and serve to protect them from snow, rain, and wind. The undercoat layer is thick and soft, which provides warmth.

Chickadees are adaptive and can survive cold winter conditions.

Black capped chickadees are amazing tiny birds that adapt to winter and do not migrate. They can survive the cold, thanks to their thick insulating feathers. They will shiver to create heat and fluff up their feathers to trap the heat close to their bodies to stay warm. They are active all winter, looking for food and retrieving food they have stashed away during the fall. They have an incredible memory and can remember thousands of spots where they have hidden their food.

Groundhog will wake in February to make the spring weather prediction.

Groundhogs hibernate in underground dens during the winter. To prepare for hibernation, groundhogs will build up their fat reserves in the fall. During hibernation, they do not eat, their breathing and heart rate decrease and they can lose up to half their body weight by the end of hibernation.

Every year on February 2nd is Groundhog Day. People believe that groundhogs can predict the arrival of spring. On the morning of Groundhog Day, a groundhog will appear from its den. If it sees its shadow, it will mean that there will be six more weeks of winter. If it can't see its shadow, then spring will arrive early.

Animals have different traits and skills for winter survival.

But they're all the same because they can't wait for spring's arrival.

If you enjoyed this book, please take a few moments
to write an honest review of it on the site of purchase.
Thank you!

MORE BEST SELLING BOOKS
BY L.R. HANSON

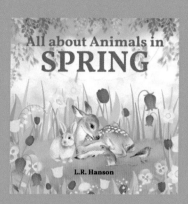

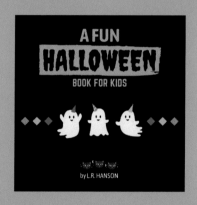

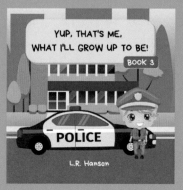

Made in the USA
Coppell, TX
01 December 2024

41438545R00021